Fairy Tales

Contents

The Fountain of Gold

Written by Malachy Doyle

Illustrated by Daniel Duncan

Page 2

The Snow Queen

Written by Smriti Prasadam-Halls

Illustrated by Ruth Hammond

Page 12

All About Snow

Written by Holly Bennet

Page 22

The Fountain of Gold

Written by Malachy Doyle

Illustrated by Daniel Duncan

Part 1

Deep in the forest, a wild man guarded a fountain that ran with liquid gold. The man was as tall as a tree, with hair down to his knees, and a body like rusty iron.

A young prince who was riding through the woods came across him. "Who are you?" he asked.

"I'm Iron John," boomed the man. "And everyone is afraid of me!"

"I'm not afraid of anyone," said Prince Hal. "Let's be friends."

So they sat and talked, and Iron John, enjoying the company of the young prince, became less wild for a while.

Later, while Iron John was sleeping, the prince dipped a flask into the golden waters of the fountain. As Hal reached in, water splashed his hair and turned it to gold.

When Iron John woke, he roared,
"You stole some of my gold!"
"I didn't," lied Prince Hal.

"I can see it in your hair!" cried
the wild man. "For that, I banish you
from your homeland!" He took
Hal's flask of gold, his horse, and
all his princely goods, and sent
him on his way.

Hiding his hair under an old
cap, the prince walked for a
day and a night, until he came
to a palace.

"I'm a poor boy," he told
the guard, "looking for work
and somewhere to stay."

"Well, Princess Daisy needs
someone to tend her flowers,"
said the man.

So the young prince became
a gardener.

Prince Hal found that he very much liked working with flowers, but when a fiery dragon came stalking the land, he decided to help. "How can I fight him, though? I have no sword or armour."

Iron John, in his magic fountain, was watching over Hal. Although Hal had tried to steal some gold, Iron John remembered how friendly the young prince had been to him. So, in the night, he left Hal a sword and a suit of armour.

Prince Hal rode off to fight the mighty dragon. The battle was long, hard and very, very hot, but at last he triumphed.

"We will have a ball to celebrate!" cried the Princess in her palace. "I will throw flowers into the air, and whoever catches them, I will dance with for the rest of the night." For she had seen the mysterious young knight, and he was the one she wished to dance with.

Part 2

So Prince Hal went to the dance, still dressed as a knight, and caught the beautiful flowers.

"Now you must take off your helmet," said Princess Daisy, smiling at him, "so I can see who you really are."

The prince, still ashamed that he had tried to steal some of Iron John's gold, couldn't bear to let anyone see his hair. "I'm sorry, but I can't," he said, running off. The princess ordered her guards to find him, but no-one could.

Iron John came to her the following morning.

"Who are you?" asked Princess Daisy.

"Iron John," said the man. "But you need not fear me …"

"I'm not afraid of anyone," said the princess.

"That's what the young prince said," said Iron John, a smile cracking his rusty old face. "I know where your mysterious knight is," he said, leading her to the garden and nodding towards the scruffy gardener.

"But that's just some boy!" cried Princess Daisy.

"Yes, but he's really a prince," said the wild man, before disappearing. "A prince with golden hair."

The princess took an apple and threw it at the young gardener.

"Oi!" cried the prince, as his cap went flying and his golden hair was revealed.

"Are you really the one who slayed the dragon?" asked Princess Daisy, with a laugh. "And are you really a prince?"

"I am," said Prince Hal, for it was time to tell the truth and put the past behind him. He told her all about the magic fountain, and how Iron John had banished him from his homeland for stealing his gold.

"But you're a hero now," said Princess Daisy, "and Iron John isn't cross with you anymore."

"Really?" said the prince.

"Yes, really," said the princess. She took him by the hand and danced among the daffodils. "I love my flowers," she said, "and I like you all the more because you love them too."

"I do," said Prince Hal, and then he looked her in the eyes and knew what came next. "Will you marry me?" he asked.

"I will," replied Princess Daisy.

Of course, Iron John came to the wedding. Only he was no longer made of iron …

"So you are just John, now?" the prince asked. "I'm sorry for stealing your gold."

"Well, I'm sorry for banishing you," said Iron John. "You were a friend to me, even just for a few hours … and though the temptation of my gold was too much for you, I knew you were good at heart."

"Is that why you helped me?" asked Prince Hal.

"It is," said Iron John, "and helping you has helped me – for the magic spell I was under has now been broken, and I have become human again."

And they danced, all three, among the daffodils.

The Snow Queen

Written by Smriti Prasadam-Halls

Illustrated by Ruth Hammond

Part 1

Long, long ago, a goblin made a magical glass mirror. This mirror didn't show things as they really were. It made anything ugly look more horrible and it made anything beautiful appear ugly.

The goblin was delighted with his mirror but one day, it slipped from his hands and shattered into a million tiny pieces that were blown across the earth. Even though the mirror was broken, each tiny sparkling crystal held the mirror's dreadful power within it. For if the smallest speck of the glass fluttered into a person's eye, everything they saw would be twisted and horrible. If the tiniest splinter entered their heart, their heart would become as cold as ice …

In a town there lived a girl
named Gerda and a boy named
Kay who were the very best of
friends. On bright summer days,
they played in the warm sunshine
while looking after the lovely
roses in Gerda's garden. On icy
winter evenings they sat in the
firelight, listening to the stories
that Gerda's grandmother told.

One such tale was about the lonely Snow Queen. She hid among snowflakes and peeped in at people's windows, looking for a child to take north with her, to keep her company in her ice palace. The story made Gerda and Kay shiver, but Gerda's grandmother comforted them. "If your heart is good and true, you have nothing to fear from the Snow Queen. Her powers can never harm you."

One bright
morning, Gerda
and Kay were playing
when suddenly Kay cried
out. He clutched his eye
and then his chest. "What's
wrong?" cried Gerda in alarm.

Roughly, Kay brushed
away Gerda's help. "I'm fine,"
he said unkindly.

But he was quite changed.

From that moment on, everything that
Kay saw appeared twisted and horrible and
his heart became cruel and cold. He made fun
of Gerda and no longer played with her. Instead,
he hurtled thoughtlessly round the village square
on his sledge.

No one realised that a small speck of the goblin's
glass mirror had entered Kay's eye, and a tiny
splinter had become caught in his heart.

That winter, in a flurry of snowflakes, a beautiful sleigh appeared on the square. Kay was mesmerised. The mysterious rider brought the sleigh to a standstill and stepped out. Kay looked up into her face and shivered.

"Why don't you sit with me?" asked the rider. She swept Kay into the sleigh and wrapped him in furs. Then she smiled at Kay and kissed his forehead.

Instantly, Kay forgot all about his home and about his friend, Gerda. His cold heart became colder still but he didn't care. For, as the snow swirled and sparkled all around him, in Kay's eyes shone the cold clear reflection of the Snow Queen.

Part 2

The bitter winter passed and Kay did not return home, but Gerda didn't give up hope. On the first morning of spring, she skipped to the river's edge and tossed in her new red shoes. She believed that the river had taken away her friend and hoped, in exchange for her shoes, that the river would tell her where it had taken Kay. Alas, her shoes were returned so she climbed into a boat and tried again. This time her shoes floated away – and so did Gerda! For the boat slipped from the river bank and carried Gerda downstream, further and further away from home.

"Oh! Maybe the river will take me to Kay," Gerda thought.

With bare and blistered feet, Gerda searched the earth for Kay. Over months and months, she took many risks and faced many dangers. Just as she was losing hope, she befriended a wild girl who was able to tell Gerda that Kay was in the ice palace of the Snow Queen. Gerda's great love for Kay moved the wild girl so much, she gave Gerda her reindeer to ride all the way to the Snow Queen's palace.

Outside the palace, a vicious wind
blew and the snowflakes formed into
fierce serpents and huge spiked monsters.
The icy creatures rose up against Gerda, but
she wasn't afraid. She had come this far, alone
and without so much as a pair of shoes upon her feet.
She whispered her grandmother's words: "If your heart
is good and true, you have nothing to fear ..."
It was all the strength she needed to
overcome the snow beasts.

Inside the palace, in the centre of the hall, sat Kay, almost blue with cold. He had been so enchanted by the Snow Queen that now his heart was almost entirely ice. He sat, trying to form ice letters into a word.

"Find the right word and you shall be free," the Snow Queen had laughed as she swept away on another journey. Kay knew it was pointless, for he had no feelings or thoughts of his own. Still, he moved the letters uselessly, this way and that.

Suddenly Gerda was there, her arms wrapped tightly round Kay. Full of pity at the sight of her dear friend she began to weep hot tears. The tears trickled over Kay, melting his frozen heart and dislodging the glass splinter. Kay saw Gerda and his eyes filled with tears which washed away the remaining speck of glass. At last he could see clearly.

The children danced for joy, scattering the ice letters across the floor. Each one fell neatly into place, spelling the word FOREVER. Kay gasped. He had his freedom!

Hand in hand, Gerda and Kay left the palace of the Snow Queen forever. They reached home older and wiser than when they left. And they smiled, for it was summer, and the roses bloomed once more in the glow of the warm sunshine.

All About Snow

Written by Holly Bennett

That's Deep! Snow Records

The UK doesn't usually get a lot of snow but in 1947, 2.1 metres lay in the Forest of Teesdale in County Durham. That's higher than most grown-ups!

The deepest snow ever measured was in the mountains of California (USA) in 1911: 11.5 metres – that's higher than *five* grown-ups!!

Walking on Snow

It's hard to walk in deep snow. One step, and you can sink up to your waist. Snowshoes were invented over 4,000 years ago. They keep you on top of the snow by spreading your weight over a wide, flat area.

The Canada lynx has built-in snowshoes – its big wide feet do the job!

Published by Pearson Education Limited, 80 Strand, London, WC2R 0RL.

www.pearsonschools.co.uk

Text © Pearson Education Limited 2016
Designed by Bigtop Design Ltd

Original illustrations © Pearson Education Limited 2016
Illustrated by Daniel Duncan and Ruth Hammond

First published 2016

20 19 18 17 16
10 9 8 7 6 5 4 3 2 1

British Library Cataloguing in Publication Data
A catalogue record for this book is available from the British Library

ISBN 978 0 435 17963 2

Printed in the UK by Ashford Colour Press

Acknowledgements

The publisher would like to thank the following individuals and organisations for their kind permission to reproduce photographs:

(Key: b-bottom; c-centre; l-left; r-right; t-top)

Alamy Images: Frank Pali / All Canada Photos 22bl; **Fotolia.com**: 6okean 22cr; **Shutterstock.com**: 2happy 22-23c, Kichigan 22-23

Cover image: Alamy Images: Frank Pali / All Canada Photos

All other images © Pearson Education

Snowflake Science

A snowflake forms in a cloud. It is an ice crystal, or a few ice crystals stuck together. The snowflakes we know best look like lacy six-pointed stars, but they come in other shapes too. Some are shaped like long tubes, or triangles.

DID YOU KNOW?
The largest snowflake ever found was bigger than a dinner plate!

In nature, snowflakes are like finger prints; no two are exactly alike. However, in a laboratory, scientists can sometimes grow snowflakes that are very hard to tell apart.

23